Name

Birthday

Place of Birth

Where do you live now?

MW01113374

How many miles are you

from your birthplace?

Where was or is your favorite place to live?

Where is most of your family?

What are your

five greatest achievements?

What is your favorite food?

What is your favorite drink?

Where is your favorite vacation site?

Describe your most brave moment.

What are five

characteristics that describe you?

What was your favorite childhood candy?

What was your favorite childhood game?

What was your favorite childhood activity?

Who was your childhood best friend?

What quality has shaped your life the most?

What quality would you give your parents credit for giving you?

What quality did you admire most in your mother and father?

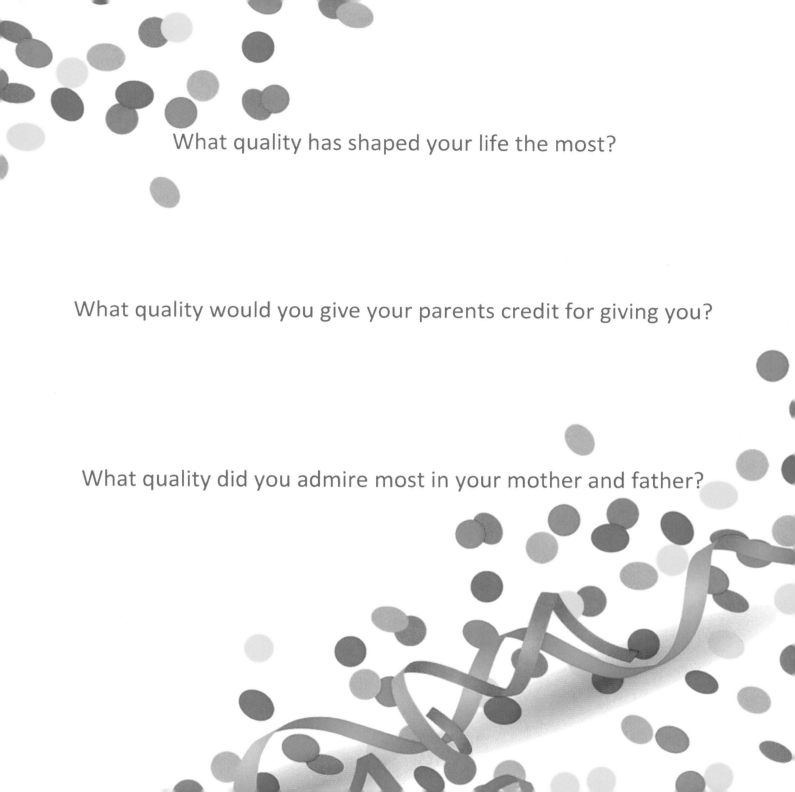

What did you want to be when you grew up?

What did you become when you did grow up?

What influenced you most for your life's work?

Do you wish you had chosen a different career/path?

What do you love most about what you do?

What would you change about what you do/your career?

What makes you most content?

If you could change one thing about the world today, what would you change?

If you could change one thing about yourself, what would you change?

If you could change one thing about another person, what would you change?

If you could go anywhere right now, where would you go?

If you could live anywhere for one year, where would you choose to live?

Do you like your name?

Do you know what your name means?

What would you name yourself?

Why?

Who is your favorite famous person?

And why?

What would you talk about with this person if you had one day to spend with him/her?

If you could give one thing to the world today, what would you give?

If you could give one thing to a family member, what would you give?

If you could give one thing to another person, what would you give?

If you could send anyone anywhere right now, where would you send him?

If you could give one possession (that belongs to you) to someone, which would you choose to give?

What were the greatest gifts you have received in your life?

Describe a perfect day in your life.

What hardship made you stronger and why?

Where were you educated in your Elementary years?

Where were you educated in your Middle School years?

Where were you educated in your High School years?

Where did you spend your years after High School?

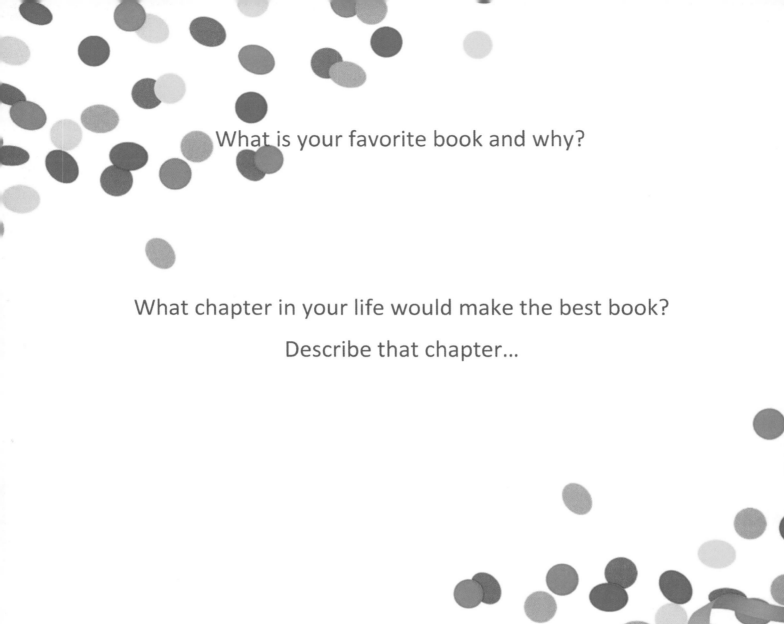

What is your favorite book and why?

What chapter in your life would make the best book?

Describe that chapter...

Family History

Ancestors: Paternal

Ancestors: Maternal

Great Grand Parents:

Origin, Birth Place and Years

Grand Parents

Origin, Birth Place and Years

Parents:

Origin, Birth Place and Years

Siblings

Origin, Birth Place and Years

Uncles and Aunts

Origin, Birth Place and Years

Cousins

Origin, Birth Place and Years

Your Children

Origin, Birth Place and Years

Grandchildren and Great Grandchildren

Origin, Birth Place and Years

Have you ever left a time capsule anywhere?

If so, what was in it?

If not, what would you have placed into one?

What advice would you give your children?

What advice would you give to your friends?

What plans do you have for the coming year?

What plans and dreams do you have for the next five years?

If you could write a prayer, a blessing, a well-wish, what would you like it to say:

My Birthday Celebration

Location of Celebration

Special Details of My Celebration

Date

Attendees at My Birthday Celebration

_____

_____

_____

_____

_____

_____

_____

_____

_____

_____

_____

_____

_____

_____

Notes and Messages from Family and Friends

_____

_____

_____

_____

_____

_____

_____

_____

_____

_____

_____

_____

_____

68098681R00024